The Culture of Japan

Rosie McCormick

Core Knowledge®

Printed in Canada

ISBN: 978-1-68380-448-2

The Culture of Japan

Table of Contents

CHAPTER 1

A Nation of Islands

Japan is a country in Asia made up of thousands of islands. On many of the islands there are mountains, thick forests, and fields of rice. Japan's nearest neighbors are Russia, China, and North and South Korea.

Japan has four *main* islands. These main islands are Hokkaido, Honshu, Shikoku, and Kyushu. Honshu is the largest island and is sometimes called the mainland.

Tokyo is the capital of Japan. It is also the largest and busiest city in Japan. Tokyo is on the island of Honshu. Other big cities are Osaka, Nagoya, and Sapporo. In terms of numbers of people, Japan has the eleventh largest population in the world. Most people in Japan speak Japanese.

Japan's national flag is a white rectangle with a red circle in the middle. The circle represents the sun because the name Japan means "the land of the rising sun." The sun rises in the east, and Japan is the easternmost country in Asia. So the rising sun appears there first.

The highest mountain in Japan is Mount Fuji. The peak of Mount Fuji is so high that the snow at the top never melts. But Mount Fuji is not just a mountain. It is also an active volcano. There are many other active volcanoes in Japan.

Japan is home to wonderful wildlife and nature. It is perhaps most known for its macaque monkeys and red-crowned cranes. The Japanese macaque is also known as the snow monkey. These monkeys have a red face and long fingers with sharp nails. The red-crowned crane is an important symbol in Japan. It can mean long life and good luck.

In Japan, there is a small cat called an Iriomote that is related to the leopard. The cat gets its name because it only lives in the forests on Iriomote Island. Although it is related to the leopard, it is about the size of a house cat.

Most of the land in Japan is either forest or mountains, so there is less space for farming. Because there is little space for farmland, fish are an important food. In the waters near Japan, there are cold and warm water currents that make it a great place for fishermen. Today, Japanese fishing ships use large nets and special equipment to bring in huge catches of fish. Fishermen do have to be careful not to overfish though!

Although farmers in Japan have little space to grow many different crops, or to graze animals, they do grow a lot of rice and vegetables. Rice is grown in paddy fields. Japanese people have grown rice for more than two thousand years. In fact, Japanese people eat rice almost every day.

CHAPTER
2

Modern Japan

Japan is a very successful, rich country. Japan makes cars, electronics such as televisions and cell phones, and steel. These things are sold all over the world. Japan is also very involved in medical research and the fight against certain diseases.

The currency, or money, that is used in Japan is called the yen. The word *yen* means circle or round object.

Japan's cities have giant glass and steel skyscrapers. These tall buildings are not just places where people work; some people live in them too. Because there is less land to build houses, most people in Japan live in apartments.

In the cities, many people travel on the underground subway system. Superfast bullet trains zip across the country. They go at speeds of up to two hundred miles per hour.

Japan is one of the world leaders in making robots that can be used in factories, offices, restaurants, hotels, stores, and even in people's homes. There are pet robots and even teacher robots!

There are robots in museums too. This robot is teaching about dinosaurs.

Like the United States, Japan has three branches of government. The political party that wins the most seats gets to be in charge of the government. This means that the leading members of the government, including the prime minister, are elected by the people.

As well as an elected government, Japan has an emperor. The emperor is called the head of state. There have been emperors in Japan for more than two thousand years.

Just like in the United States, children in Japan go to school five days a week. Japanese children learn such things as math, science, computer science, Japanese, English, history, art, and music. At lunchtime, children eat in their classrooms, and they take turns serving one another.

Earthquakes happen a lot in Japan. In fact, there are more than fifteen hundred each year. Even though buildings are made extra strong, sometimes they are damaged in a strong earthquake.

Because there are so many earthquakes, children have regular earthquake drills at school, and people practice how to keep safe in their homes.

Baseball is a popular sport in Japan. The Yomiuri Giants are one of the top baseball teams.

Sumo wrestling is an important sport that dates back more than one thousand years. Sumo wrestlers oil and comb their hair to look like a ginkgo tree leaf.

Martial arts such as karate and judo date back to when Japanese warriors were specially trained to fight for the local leaders they served. People today still learn these special skills.

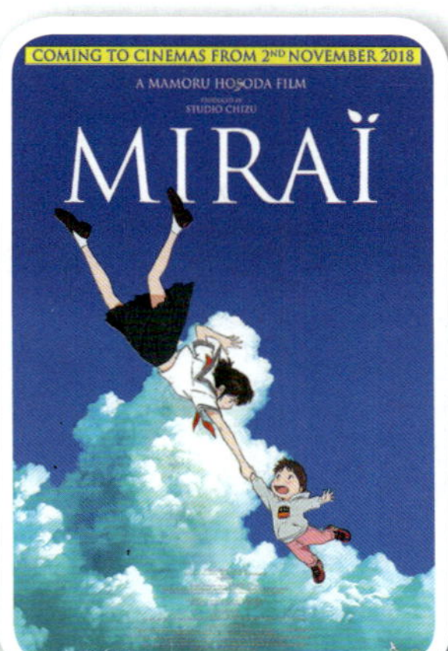

Japanese people love to read comic books and watch cartoons.

CHAPTER
3

Japanese Art and Traditions

Japan has an ancient culture that stretches back for thousands of years. Long ago, rulers lived in castles, and soldiers fought to defend them and their land. Himeji Castle, also known as White Heron Castle, was built in the 1300s. The castle has eighty-three rooms and is the most visited castle in Japan.

Japanese is a spoken and written language. It is probably difficult to learn to write Japanese because it is written using three types of scripts, each with different characters. And the Japanese do not use spaces between words!

Kimonos are traditional, silk robes. Long ago, women and girls had special kimonos for certain occasions. The color or pattern of a kimono would show what the occasion was. For example, kimonos with flowers would be worn in spring. Today, kimonos are mostly worn at weddings, funerals, and special holidays.

The Japanese tea ceremony is an important Japanese tradition. Green tea is prepared, served, and drunk in a certain way. Traditionally, a tea ceremony happens in or near a garden.

November 15 is a special day for children in Japan. It is called *Shichi-go-san*, which means "seven, five, three." If you are seven, five, or three years old, then this is your holiday! Parents take their children who have reached these ages to the temple to pray for health and happiness.

Children learn origami in school. Origami is the ancient art of folding paper into shapes, such as animals or things found in nature. The word *origami* means paper folding, and people in Japan have been doing it for hundreds of years. Origami was once used in religious ceremonies. Today, it is a popular hobby.

Flower arranging, or ikebana, is very popular in Japan. To do it correctly, there are many rules to follow. For example, there are set numbers of branches and flowers for certain kinds of arrangements. Stems arranged a certain way might represent mountains. The petals of an open flower might be a pond.

Another popular art in Japan is bonsai. Bonsai is the art of growing miniature trees. There are lots of rules to follow here too. Bonsai trees can live for hundreds of years.

Every spring in Japan, people spend time admiring the beautiful cherry blossoms that bloom for a short time. There are flower-watching parties, picnics, and celebrations. Long ago, the arrival of the cherry blossom was a sign that it was the beginning of the rice-planting season.

Haiku is a traditional form of Japanese poetry. In a haiku poem, there can only be three lines with a set number of syllables. Line one has five syllables, line two has seven syllables, and line three has five syllables. This haiku was written hundreds of years ago by the Japanese poet Matsuo Basho.

Japanese artists have a long tradition of painting nature scenes. Often these scenes have included, birds, plants, water, and landscapes. One of Japan's most famous pieces of art was actually created on painted woodblocks by the artist Hokusai. It is called *The Great Wave off Kanagawa*.

Core Knowledge®

CKHG™

Core Knowledge History and Geography™

Series Editor-in-Chief

E. D. Hirsch Jr.

Editorial Directors

Linda Bevilacqua and Rosie McCormick

Subject Matter Expert

Yongguang Hu, PhD, Department of History, James Madison University

Illustration and Photo Credits

Aflo Co. Ltd. / Alamy Stock Photo: 11b, 12b
Anthony Shaw / Alamy Stock Photo: 7b
BFA / Alamy Stock Photo: 15c
Buyenlarge / SuperStock: 24
CBW / Alamy Stock Photo: 9b
David Warren / Alamy Stock Photo: Cover D, 4
Eddie Gerald / Alamy Stock Photo: 14b
FLORA / Alamy Stock Photo: 21b
Gavin Hellier / Alamy Stock Photo: 6a
Henry Westheim Photography / Alamy Stock Photo: 15a
Hideo Kurihara / Alamy Stock Photo: 5
ImageBROKER / Alamy Stock Photo: 18a, 18b, 22
ITAR-TASS News Agency / Alamy Stock Photo: 9a
Karen Kasmauski / SuperStock: 8
Luciano Mortula / Alamy Stock Photo: 16
Mauritius images GmbH / Alamy Stock Photo: i, iii, 19, 20b
Mint Images Limited / Alamy Stock Photo: 13, 21a
NHPA / SuperStock: Cover C, 6b
Nobuo Matsumura / Alamy Stock Photo: 6c
Nuttawut Uttamaharad / Alamy Stock Photo: 10b
Pacific Press Service / Alamy Stock Photo: 14a
Philippe Michel / age fotostock / SuperStock: Cover A, 2b
Photo Japan / Alamy Stock Photo: Cover B, 15d
Sean Pavone / Alamy Stock Photo: 3, 10a
SOURCENEXT / Alamy Stock Photo: 20a
Thomas Kyhn Rovsing Hjørnet / Alamy Stock Photo: 17
ton koene / Alamy Stock Photo: 11a, 12a
Wolfgang Kaehler / SuperStock: 7a
ZUMA Press, Inc. / Alamy Stock Photo: 15b